Easy-to-U

Evangelistic
Sermon Outlines

compiled by

Charles R. Wood

KREGEL PUBLICATIONS
Grand Rapids, Michigan 49501

Introduction

Evangelism is at the core of the proper business of the church of Jesus Christ. The fantastic proportions of the current day population explosion give new meaning to the old adage, "evangelize or die." Unless the church turns its attention to the centricity of this imperative, Christianity may well diminish into an imperceptable minority within three generations.

The sermon outlines included in this book are designed to assist the man who is interested in evangelizing. They are designed to have an appeal to the lost, both an emotional and a volitional appeal. There is some food for the saints here, but the primary thrust of this particular book is assistance for the soul-winning pastor as he mounts his pulpit.

Once again the sermons are drawn from a number of sources. About one-half are the product of the editor's own preaching ministry. These may be marked by the absence of any citation at the close of the sermon. The remainder have been drawn from a wide variety of preachers. It has been the attempt of the editor to include only those sermons which are sufficiently up-to-date in their approach as to be readily adaptable to the present day. Of necessity, this involves the exclusion of many otherwise splendid homiletical contributions. So be it, for our purpose is practical rather than sentimental or demonstrative.

The sermons included are designed to be preached. That means that the outlines are such that they may be used "as is" or they may be expanded and adapted to give play to the user's own style and background. It should go without saying in a book of this nature, but it bears repeating - before any of these sermons are preached, relevant scriptures ought to be carefully read and studied. A tremendous amount of "meat" may be grafted upon the bones of an outline by a careful consideration of the Biblical text.

The conviction that the Word of God never returns to Him void but always accomplishes its purpose is one that underlies the ministry — both spoken and written — of the editor. In the light of this conviction, this work is sent forth with full confidence in the power of the Spirit of God to make men "wise unto salvation" and with the earnest prayer that the sermons contained in it will be used by the Spirit of God to accomplish that purpose.

Contents

Textual Index

The Peace That The Saviour Can Give
JOHN 14:27

Introduction:

There is more talk about peace and less peace than ever before. This is true in the personal as well as the international and national realms. The only real peace available anywhere today is the peace which Christ gives.

I. **The Gift - Peace**
   A. Note its nature:
      1. It is not the absence of strife or merely smooth interpersonal relationships.
      2. It is an inner state of calm and order which will affect both the inner man and interpersonal relationships.
   B. Note its quality: it is connected with Christ and it touches into the spiritual realm.

II. **The Giver - Christ**
   A. There is a real contrast here:
      1. Christ's peace - real, delivered on promise and continuing.
      2. The world's peace - unreal, undependable and temporary.
   B. The character of Christ's peace:
      1. The same peace He knew is what He gives.
      2. For Him it involved calm in turmoil, steadiness of purpose, rightness with the Father and the quiet confidence of full trust.

III. **The Giving**
   A. It is a gift - that means that it is received rather than earned or worked up. This contrasts with so many other religious philosophies.
   B. There is a marked contrast in giving:
      1. Christ gives fully, freely and finally.
      2. The world gives grudgingly (have to work for it), halfheartedly and occassionally.

IV. **The Goal Of The Giving**
   A. "Let not your heart be troubled"
      1. Do not let yourself be continually stirred up.
      2. Know peace in the midst of strife.
   B. "Neither let it be afraid"

7

1. Do not allow fear to grip your heart.
2. Do not allow apprehension to take control of you.

Conclusion:

There isn't much real peace in the world today. The only genuine peace is that which the Lord Jesus Christ can bring. This peace is brought only to those who receive Him and the peace He brings with Him when He comes into a life.

Redemption

EPHESIANS 1:7

Introduction:

In verse 3 we are told that we have been "blessed with all spiritual blessings." The following verses detail some of the blessings we have received in Him. We are told about election, predestination, adoption, acceptance, and now, redemption. Although the word is frequently used, it is often used without understanding. Here is an attempt to explain its meaning and significance.

I. **Its Nature**
   A. Definition: setting free a person or thing which has come to belong to another.
   B. It is beautifully illustrated in Leviticus 25:47-49.
   C. Its explanation is simple:
      1. The term which describes the act by which God sets free sinners.
      2. Bound up with salvation but technically separate.

II. **Its Method - "Through His Blood"**
   This tells us how redemption is secured:
   A. Man belonged to God by creation but was taken by Satan because of sin.
   B. In order for man to be set free, sin must be paid for.
   C. Only blood can pay off sin according to the Bible (Hebrews 9:22). Blood stands for death, and the fact that death is required to pay for sin shows that sin is not to be treated lightly.
   D. Christ paid the price required by giving His life.

III. **Its Price - "The Blood"**
   A. Redemption is secured at the price of the life of Christ.
   B. We stand in awe at being the beneficiaries of something which cost the very life of the Son of God.

IV. **Its Benefits**
   A. A setting free:
      1. From sin, bondage and corruption.
      2. To Christ and a new life in Him.
   B. Forgiveness.

V. Its Source (How May One Secure It?)

A. Redemption is not just by or through Christ, but it is *in* Him.

B. Redemption comes by means of union with His person. This in turn comes through faith in Him.

Conclusion:

When Christ shed His blood to provide redemption, your freedom was part of what He purchased. Have you accepted the freedom which He bought for you?

Something New
II CORINTHIANS 5:17

Introduction:

All of us enjoy some new belongings once in a while. Most of these, however, are perishable and soon pass away. God wants us to have something permanent and lasting --- a new heart.

I. **The Old Creation (The "Old" Man Or The "Natural" Man.)**
   A. This man has an evil heart and a sinful nature. This is amply illustrated by current events and self-examination.
   B. This man is alienated from God by sin, resulting in unrest, etc.
   C. This man has a low set of values arising out of a distorted mind. His value system is based on something other than the revealed will of God.
   D. This man has a stunted and stulted life. He is unhappy, purposeless and doomed even though he may claim to be happy.

II. **The New Creation**
   A. This man has a new nature and a new heart. Desires, inner life and outlook are all changed.
   B. This man is in fellowship with God both within now and in reality for all eternity.
   C. This man has a high set of values arising out of the revealed word of God. He patterns his life after a perfect pattern and therefore is not dependent upon his own thinking or the thinking of others for his standard.
   D. This man has a new life. Old things are passed, and new things are in their place in a positive and satisfactory life.

III. **The Re-Creation**
   A. The change between the old and the new is the result of a new relationship, described as "in Christ".
      1. The man has received Christ as his Saviour.
      2. He is now related to God through Christ.
   B. The change is open to all who desire it.
      1. All need it according to the Bible and experience.
      2. The choice comes to rest with the individual and

what he will do with it.

C. The change is easily available. All one has to do is confess sin and ask God for His salvation. He has promised to save anyone who calls upon Him for that salvation.

Conclusion:

One of the great truths of Christianity is that it can effect tremendous change in the lives of people. Have you gotten something permanently new in your life? God can give it to you if you will come and seek it.

The Publican In The Temple
LUKE 18:13 & 14

Introduction:

This is a well-known story that teaches so much spiritual truth. In few places in Scripture do we find the hearts of men so clearly revealed as we do here. In few places do we see men for what they really are as we do here.

As we observe this story and the words of the publican in particular, we are reminded of several things:

I. A Conviction Of Personal Guilt

A. The publican prayed, "God be merciful to me *a sinner.*" He thus showed that he saw himself as he really was.

B. The convincing ministry of the Holy Spirit is needed to give us a true understanding of our state in the sight of God.

II. A Passionate Grief On Account Of Sin

A. This was demonstrated by the publican when he "smote upon his breast."

B. This grief was the result of:

1. The deep offense he had offered to God. He recognized that his sin was against God and in the sight of God.
2. The awful injury he had inflicted upon himself. In sinning against God, we are actually damaging our own souls.
3. The hurtful influence he had exerted on others. No man sins unto himself; the consequences of his sins almost always affect others.

III. A Deep Humility Mingled With Shame Before God

A. He showed this by standing afar off. He didn't want to get too close lest his presence corrupt that which was holy.

B. He showed this in his unwillingness to so much as lift up his eyes to heaven as he prayed.

IV. An Earnest Prayer To Heaven

A. Notice the object of that prayer - "mercy." From justice he could expect nothing but punishment.

B. Notice the character of his prayer.

1. It was simple and brief denoting earnestness and sincerity.

2. It was presented in the way that God had dictated — in the temple at the time of prayer.

V. A Happy Result

    A. "This man went down to his house justified rather than the other." He came up lowly and went back exalted.

    B. The Pharisee came up proudly and went back without having found that for which he came in the first place.

Conclusion:

This story is actually in accord with much of the teaching of other places in Scripture. "Thus saith the Lord, the High and Holy One that inhabiteth eternity, whose name is holy, I dwell in the high and holy place; with him also that is of a contrite and humble spirit, to revive the spirit of the humble and to revive the heart of the contrite one."

- Adapted from *Sketches of Revival Sermons*

The Life-Look

ISAIAH 45:22

Introduction:

People are looking everywhere today to find salvation and peace. They look everywhere but to the true source of forgiveness, the only available source of peace and salvation. peace and salvation.

I. What Does It Mean To Look To God?
A. It involves the admission that there is a God.
B. It involves speaking to the God who has been admitted, telling Him about the soul and its condition.
C. It involves being sure it is God who is contacted rather than some substitute:
  1. Some substitute a crucifix.
  2. Some substitute the Bible itself, thus giving the Bible the place of prominence that God is to have.
D. It involves recognition that the only source of salvation is God Himself.

II. For What Part Of Salvation Are We To Look To God?
A. For the pardon of all our sin.
B. For newness of life.
C. For keeping and perfecting power in life.
D. In short, for all of salvation.

III. What Is Our Encouragement To Look To God?
A. It is God's command - "look unto me . . . "
B. It is God's promise - "be ye saved . . . " As surely as one looks, one shall be saved.
C. It is based upon His Godhead - "I am God." There is nothing outside the scope of His power.
D. It is based upon the character of God.

IV. What Is The Best Time To Look To The Lord?
A. The best time is God's time - today.
B. The present time is the only time you have.

Conclusion:

If you are looking for something worthwhile in life to give you peace, security and assurance, look to the Lord Jesus Christ and the salvation which God has provided in Him.

- Adapted from C. H. Spurgeon

Have You Heard The News?

LUKE 2:6-11

Introduction:

This is an everyday expression. When two men meet, one says, "Have you heard the news?" In the Scripture passage the angel said, "fear not . . . good tidings." The word "tidings" means "news." In this message there is good news for bad people and bad news for good people.

I. There Is Bad News For Good People

A. Some think it is good enough to be good when it comes to salvation.

B. Most men expect to go to heaven because they are good men.

C. To those who are trusting in being good there is bad news:

1. Christ said, "I came not to call righteous, but sinners . . . "

2. Paul said, "There is none righteous, no not one."

3. Paul also said, " . . . all have sinned and come short of the glory . . . "

4. Christ said, "Except a man be born again . . . "

II. There Is Good News For Bad People

A. Good people are not saved because they are good.

B. Bad people do not go to hell because they are bad.

C. Listen to the good news:

1. Christ came to save sinners.

2. Christ died for the ungodly.

3. They that believe are justified.

D. Do something about the good news.

1. Confess the fact that you are a bad person.

2. Receive Christ as personal Saviour.

Conclusion:

Good news for the bad; bad news for the good. All news from Christ.

Forgiveness and Fear
PSALM 130:4

Introduction:

How wonderful to be forgiven! Those who labor under the weight of guilt for sin or harm done in the past often cry out to know the meaning of real forgiveness. God offers this forgiveness. Even though others may not be willing to forgive, God is willing to do so.

I. A Most Cheering Announcement
   A. It is most certainly true.
   B. It is consistent with God's very nature to forgive.
   C. God has given the best pledge of forgiveness possible by giving His Son for us.
   D. We have numerous promises of forgiveness as well as the gift of His Son.
   E. The very essence of the Gospel includes the proclamation of forgiveness of sins:
      1. Many testimonies bear this out.
      2. This is the whole point of the Gospel.
   F. This statement is in the present tense which adds to its worth.
   G. The forgiveness is with God Himself.
   H. This forgiveness is unlimited in its character.
   I. This forgiveness is as complete as it could possibly be.

II. A Most Admirable Design
   A. God's design in providing forgiveness is quite contrary to what some have said and thought:
      1. Some use His willingness to forgive as an excuse to continue sinning or to postpone a decision for Christ to a later time.
      2. Some say, "there is forgiveness; let us keep on sinning."
      3. Some say that it is too simple. If men can have pardon simply by believing in Jesus, then they will lose all restraint. Let us rather keep men under the thumb by forcing them to perform certain sacraments and penances.
   B. Here is a picture of God's design:
      1. If there were no pardon, it is quite certain that no one would fear God at all. What would be the point if there were no forgiveness anyhow?

2. If there were no pardon, there would be no one left to fear God.
3. Faithful preaching of the Gospel begets faith in the soul.
4. Faith in the soul produces repentance.
5. After repentance is produced, prayer and obedience follow hard behind.

Conclusion:

Full forgiveness is to be had from God. Why should you not have it?

- Adapted from C. H. Spurgeon

Contrition

PSALM 41:17

Introduction:

Most of David's Psalms are of a joyful character, full of exhortation, praise and thanksgiving, but this one is an exception. At the time David wrote this one, he had a heavy heart in consequence of remembered sin.

Deeply and painfully conscious of sin, David mourned his sin, all the while trusting in God's mercy. This is clear from the expressions used at the beginning and ending of the Psalm.

The only sacrifice the penitent Psalmist could offer to God was that of a broken and contrite heart, nor was such sacrifice in vain.

I. **What Is A Contrite Heart?**
   A. What it is not:
      1. It is not just a broken heart. Hearts are broken by disappointment, sorrow, losses, remorse, etc.
      2. It is not the worldly sorrow of a heart merely broken.
   B. What it is:
      1. A contrite heart is convinced of sin. Conviction is a deep sense of the evil of sin and the fact that it is against God.
      2. A truly contrite heart is truly conscious of God's righteous displeasure against sin.
         a. A sinner needs to learn to hate sin as God hates it.
         b. Every true contrite heart must become aware of God's displeasure with sin.
      3. A contrite heart is humbled before God. All pride and vain thoughts are put away, and the soul bows in humility.
      4. A contrite heart will make a sincere confession of its guilt:
         a. Confession of sin is part of true repentance.
         b. The sincerity of one's confession will determine the degree of one's contrition.
      5. A contrite heart will desire and seek divine healing. There is a difference between remorse and contrition. Remorse is sullen and hopeless. Contrition is open and hopeful.

II. How Does God Regard A Contrite Heart?

A. God has promised that He will not despise a broken and contrite heart.

B. How can we be sure that this is so?

    1. Because of His own gracious character. God is love and therefore will not spurn the sinner.

    2. Because the Word of God assures us. The Scriptures are replete with many promises of mercy to the contrite.

    3. Because we have many instances of God's mercy recorded in the Word.

        a. David Himself is a prime example.

        b. Saul of Tarsus provides another example.

Conclusion:

There is peace for the one who is burdened with sin, but that peace is reserved in the wisdom and mercy of God for those who demonstrate contrition.

Charlesworth

A Matter Of Two Ways
MATTHEW 7:13 & 14

Introduction:

In spite of all man's efforts to make it appear otherwise, there is still a matter of two options and two options only when it comes to the eternal destiny of a man and his soul. Christ made that very plain in His teaching while here on earth.

I. **The Gate Is Strait**
A. Word means "narrow" and has reference to the fact that right at the beginning Christianity is narrow.
B. This speaks of the beginning of the Christian way.
1. There is only room for one at a time so you can't crowd in with your family.
2. This also speaks of the personal nature of salvation. It is one at a time rather than part of a mass.
3. There are many things that won't fit through the gate — worldliness and selfishness, etc.
C. This runs counter to much modern thinking.
1. We tend to try to dress up Christianity to make it popular in an effort to attract converts. There is a twofold error here:
a. The Holy Spirit is supposed to attract converts.
b. The converts gotten this way usually don't last.
2. This accounts for many problems for people don't find what they expect.

II. **The Way Is Narrow**
A. It continues to be narrow after the strait gate is entered. This is "from the outset to the end."
B. There are things which make it narrow:
1. The world pushes in on either side.
2. The enemy lies in ambush on either side of the way — cares on one side and temptations on the other.
3. The old man crowds out. This is a way on which there is room for only one to walk — the old man tries to wedge in and crowd us off the path.
4. The critics with their carping and the persecutors

with their pressure both keep the way narrow as well.

C. It is important that we realize this narrowness.
 1. This will answer some of our questions of "Why, Lord?"
 2. This will keep us from discouragement.
 3. This will help us adjust our value systems.
 4. This will change our way of thinking and vitalize our lives.

III. **The Alternative Is Plain**

A. There certainly are two ways. Casual observation even makes this obvious.

B. They have contrasting popularity.
 1. The wide gate and way is popular. Actually you don't have to do anything to get on this way - just stay the way you are.
 2. The narrow gate is unpopular. This is the lonely way of the minority and few find it.

C. They have contrasting ends:
 1. Real issues focus here.
 2. The end is plain. One ends in hell; the other ends in eternal life.
 3. It is at this point that the score is equalled.

Conclusion:

There are two ways, different and contrasting, but none the less real. They demand an immediate choice. Which gate will you enter? Which way will you walk? Your eternal destiny rests upon your decision.

Signs and Spirits
MATTHEW 12:38-45

Introduction:

In spite of the enormous amount of change about us on every hand, man shows basic characteristics which are essentially unchanged from the days in which the Bible was written.

There is so little new that the very condemnation Christ spoke against His contemporaries has completely contemporary significance to our day. Note Christ's accusations and feel their contemporary sting:

I. **An Evil And Adulterous Generation**
   A. A generation occupied with evil. This is a situation which has not changed much with time.
   B. A generation involved with adultery.
      1. This is a word which refers to any type of moral unfaithfulness and may be applied to physical or spiritual realms.
      2. There was much adultery in the days of Christ, both spiritual and physical unfaithfulness.
      3. Immorality has become almost a way of life in the present day.

II. **A Sign Seeking Generation**
   A. The Pharisees were seeking a sign when they had all kinds of signs around them if they would only look.
      1. This was very common practice in His time (Matthew 16:1-4; Mark 8:11 & 12; John 2:18; 6:30).
      2. The people of His time were always seeking something spectacular.
   B. The modern generation is always seeking a sign also:
      1. The man who wants scientific proof for God is seeking a sign.
      2. The popularity of "pseudo-prophecy" is a type of sign-seeking.
      3. Much of the emphasis on the Holy Spirit is sign-seeking.

III. **A Light Rejecting Generation**
   A. Christ uses an Old Testament illustration.
      1. Queen of Sheba came to behold and believe.
      2. These men were failing to believe when faced

with the testimony of one greater than Solomon and were thus guilty of rejecting light.
B. The same thing is true today.
   1. Light is available, but men turn away and reveal more of their inherent weakness.
   2. This generation probably has as much light as any generation ever has had (films, literature, radio, etc.).

IV. A Self-Reliant Generation
A. Christ uses a parable of picturesque description which tells of a man getting rid of a demon through self-effort.
   1. When this is done, the man is worse off than he was to begin with.
   2. Application to salvation by "self-help" is obvious.
B. This is so typical of modern man.
   1. In this day of "do-it-yourself" religion ("bootstrap salvation"), there are hosts of people trying to cast out their own demons of sinfulness.
   2. The man today, as the man of old, ends up empty and drained.

Conclusion:
Christ condemns His generation for some of the same things the current generation can be condemned for. In so doing, He puts His finger on the key point - the sign of the Prophet Jonah. That sign pointed to His finished work.

Men looked and look for solutions everywhere. There are none found until men begin to look to His finished work on the cross.

From Here To Eternity
EPHESIANS 2:8-10

Introduction:

It's a familiar meal — meat, potatoes, peas and gravy. The only thing missing is the dessert. I don't know how you feel, but I like my dessert.

We quote Ephesians 2:8 & 9, and they go down like a familiar meal, a meal without dessert because we have forgotten verse 10.

Let's have a complete meal. Let's look at all three verses and see the three main streams of thought which run through them.

I. **Salvation Is Entirely Of God**
   A. "For by grace are ye saved"
      1. Grace is favor when punishment is due. It stands opposed to merit on the part of man or necessity on the part of God.
      2. The verb is in the past tense — you have been saved.
   B. "It is the gift of God"
      1. The gift referred to here is salvation.
      2. A genuine gift involves absolutely no obligation whatever. As soon as obligation enters in, it is not a true gift.
   C. "For we are His workmanship, created in Christ Jesus"
      1. Salvation involves a new creation entirely fabricated by God.
      2. We are created "in Christ Jesus". Without Him we are nothing.

II. **Man Plays Virtually No Part In Salvation**
   A. "That not of yourselves"
      1. Salvation is not of yourselves.
      2. This is an inclusive-exclusive statement. It includes absolutely everything a man might do and then turns around and excludes it.
   B. "Not of works, lest any man should boast"
      1. There is no place for works. Anything which involves human effort or participation is ruled out.
      2. There is no place for boasting. Boasting is ruled

25

out by the absence of anything a man can do. It is important that boasting be out because the end of salvation is to bring glory to God and the presence of boasting would rule out God's exclusive glory.

C. "Through faith"
   1. Believing is not a work!
   2. Faith is turning to God with a sense of need, weakness and emptiness and with a willingness to receive what He has to offer. It is not a substitute for works; it is the opposite of works.
   3. God does all the work; grace is the source. Man merely accepts; faith is the means.

III. God Has A Special Purpose In Saving Men
   A. " . . . we are . . . created . . . unto good works . . . "
      1. The primary purpose of God in saving men is holiness rather than heaven. This is why God doesn't take a man to heaven as soon as He is saved.
      2. Works come after salvation and not before. We work because we are saved, not to be saved.
   B. "Which God hath before ordained that we should walk in them."
      1. God has ordained good works and He desires that we should walk in them.
      2. It was the plan of God from the inception of salvation that we should live our lives in the performance of good works.

Conclusion:

God has a special purpose in saving men. Are you fulfilling that purpose?

Nothing man can do will earn salvation. Are you trying to earn your own?

Salvation is entirely by God. Have you received it yet?

The Mistakes Of A Rich Man

MATTHEW 19:16-22

Introduction:

There are reasons why men do not come to Christ, some of which are as old as Christianity itself.

In this story attention is usually drawn to the matter of money and possessions, but this young man had four problems which are ever so similar to the problems which keep men from Christ today.

I. He Failed To Understand Who Christ Was - "Good Master"
   A. He was sincere and seeking with a high regard for Christ.
   B. Christ's answer points up this problem: "Why do you call me good? There is only one good." Christ is either God or He is not good.
   C. The same problem exists today. Men recognize that Christ must be explained somehow, but they simply don't or won't recognize Him for what He really is. Christ is either what He claimed to be or not worth any worship.

II. He Failed To Understand Spiritual Things - "What Must I Do?"
   A. He was seeking to know what tangible action he could take to receive eternal life. (Actually "doing" and "inheriting" are contradictory.)
   B. Christ gives him the only answer possible:
      1. Quotes him the law - this is the only thing one can *do* to get eternal life.
      2. The answer was designed to show him the real meaning of the law and thus reveal to him the extent of his need.
      3. Christ used the portion of the law He did for a reason: love for man whom we can see is easy compared to love for God whom we can't see.
      4. Don't miss the fact that Christ also said, "Come and follow me."
   C. The same question comes today. Man asks, "What must I *do*?" The only answer that can be given is, "Keep the law." There is no other way in which man can *do* and be saved.

27

III. He Failed To Understand Himself - "All These Things Have I Done"

A. He was probably sincere in his answer - felt he had kept the law.

B. Christ points out to him that he has not kept the law in spite of his boast of having done so:

1. If he really understood and kept the law, he would have no problem in doing what Christ commanded him.

2. The fact that he could not part with his riches showed the extent to which he had missed the point of the law.

C. The same mistake is made today. Men won't come to Christ either because they don't think they are bad enough or because they think they have done everything which could be properly required.

IV. He Failed To Understand Proper Priorities - "He Went Away Sorrowful"

A. He comes with great interest and sincerity. He goes away without a word because of the nature of the demand.

B. Christ comments on his real problem - he is so attached to his wealth and materialism that he can't keep the law and he won't seek salvation.

C. The same problem exists today. Many people are being kept away from Christ today because they are too attached to the material things of this world.

Conclusion:

Here are four good reasons why a man wouldn't come to Christ. They are also good reasons why men don't come to Christ today.

What has kept you from coming to know Christ up to now? Is it worth it?

The Master and The Rich Young Ruler
MARK 10:17-22

Introduction:

The pages of the Bible are full of pictures of men. Many times we go to the Bible and are surprised to meet men who are so similar to men today. This is what we should expect, however, because human nature doesn't change.

In this passage we meet a man who has many counterparts today.

I. Meet The Man

A. He was young (Cf. Matthew 19:20 and Luke 18:18).

B. He was rich (Cf. Luke 18:23 and Matthew 19:23).

C. He was very moral. Notice that Christ does not question the claim he makes.

D. He was religious. The very fact that he came to Christ indicates some spiritual feelings and desires.

E. He demonstrated some promise. Mark 10:21 says that Christ "loved" him. This may well mean that Christ "desired him."

II. Examine His Problem

A. He was trusting in the wrong things - money, morality and works. (This story shows that doing good is not enough because he did a great deal of good.)

B. He lacked assurance. He was an honest seeker, but there is never any real assurance where there is not faith in the Lord.

C. He loved his money more than he desired eternal things. Although he asked about eternal things, he turned away when it became obvious that it would cost him something. (Christ likely placed this requirement in his way to show him how imperfect his professed faith and his professed concern for his fellow man really were.)

III. Give Him An Answer

A. He needed Christian contentment (Cf. I Timothy 6:6-10).

1. He could have found this in Christ.

2. It comes with a proper realization of things as they actually are.

3. Places money and morality in proper perspective.

B. He needed eternal investments (Cf. I Timothy

6:17-19).
1. He had to learn that the things of God are of first importance.
2. He had to learn that Christ and God had to be first.
3. He needed to find a life that would last beyond time.

Conclusion:

Here is the story of a man who met Christ but was kept from receiving Him by self-trust and love for material things. Today there are many people who are kept from receiving Christ by love for material things and trust in self.

The last glimpse we have of this man in the passage shows him sorrowfully walking away from Christ. Could it be that you are also walking away from Christ because of the emphasis you place upon material things or because of your trust in your own ability to please God?

Reactions To Jesus
MATTHEW 13:53-58

Introduction:

The One who had spent the first thirty years of his life in Nazareth was back from the outside world after several years away. The people of his hometown were no doubt interested in hearing this One of whom they had heard so much.

He went into the synagogue and began to teach the very people He had known since the days of His youth (likely some there that had grown up with Him). He read from the Old Testament and then commented on it. His manner and remarks caused quite a reaction.

I. Reactions To Jesus
   A. Astonishment - "they were struck with wonder":
      1. It was what He said and the way He said it.
      2. It was obvious that there was something special here.
   B. Questioning:
      1. Where did He get this wisdom and power?
      2. Isn't he just one of us here?
   C. Offended - "caused to stumble":
      1. They couldn't work out all the details so they were offended.
      2. They actually "fell over Him" as Peter says (I Peter 2:8).

II. Lessons From The Reaction To Jesus
   A. Many today are astonished by Him.
      1. Many churches where He is preached are full indicating an interest.
      2. Religious books on the best-seller list reveal interest in Him.
   B. Many have questions about Him.
      1. They don't understand everything about Him.
      2. Some, like those in Nazareth, have grown too "familiar" with Him.
   C. Many more "stumble" over Him today.
      1. Some ask too many questions - we will accept almost anything in life by faith except Jesus Christ.
      2. Some have grown far too familiar with Him.
         a. Born and raised in "Christian" homes in a

"Christian" land, they hear so much about Him that they tend to know *of* Him rather than to truly know Him.

b. Some have become so familiar with Him and His name that they fail to attach any real significance to Him or His claims.

Conclusion:

The reactions to Jesus when He returned to Nazareth are both interesting and informative. Men today react in much the same manner as these men of long ago.

The crucial question which you face is that of your reaction to Jesus.

What Think Ye Of Jesus Christ?

MATTHEW 24:42

Introduction:

Christ is in conflict with the Pharisees once again. The question comes: "What think ye of Christ?"

Christ is in the hall of judgment. The question comes: "What think ye of Christ?"

Neither the Pharisees nor Pilate had the correct answer. Do you?

I. **The Importance Of The Question**
    A. What you think of Him is a matter of life and death (note the thieves on the cross).
    B. What you think of Him will condition your understanding of the Bible.
    C. What you think of Him will condition whether or not you live forever.

II. **Some Interesting Answers To The Question**
    A. He was a good man:
       His own answer to Pilate rules this out. He was either the Son of God or a miserable liar.
    B. He was a fine moral example:
       The fact that He was more than that is revealed in His words, "I am come to *seek* and to *save* . . . "
    C. He was a demented genius:
       Nothing could be more contrary to the scope of the Biblical story or the record of the history of the church than that.
    D. He was a figment of the inflamed imagination of Paul. He has an objective existence, historically proven, totally apart from any mention or citation by the Apostle Paul.
    E. He never actually existed:
       One has to be anti-intellectual and totally in disregard of history to even suggest such a ridiculous thing.

III. **The Answer The Bible Gives To The Question**
    A. Begin by calling witnesses:
       1. David (Matthew 22:43).
       2. Paul (Romans 8:3 and 32).
       3. Roman centurian (Matthew 15:29). He is called because he was not originally "on the team."

B. Note the statement of God: "This is my beloved Son in whom I am well pleased."
C. Note the statement of Christ Himself: "Thou sayest that I am."
D. Note the facts of the case:
1. He was the Son of God.
2. He came to seek the lost.
3. He died for all men.
4. He is the Saviour of the world.

IV. The Application Of The Correct Answer
A. He died for all men and that includes you.
B. He made open the only possible way you can get to God.
C. He offers you eternal and real life.
D. You must make the decision about the matter.

Conclusion:

The most important question you will ever be asked or ever have to answer is simply this: "What think ye of Christ?"

A Matter Of Two Ways
JEREMIAH 21:8 and DEUTERONOMY 30:19

Introduction:
   God speaks to Israel and still speaks to men today with the same words and message. These were words spoken to a sinful and God-forsaking people by a longsuffering God who still speaks to sinful and God-forsaking people today.

I. Behold . . . The Way Of Life
   A. Man loves and fights for life from the baby's first gasp to the old man's dying gasp.
   B. God offers life to all.
      1. Christ possesses life in His very being. (John 1:4)
      2. Christ offers new life. (II Corinthians 5:17)
      3. Christ offers happiness in life. (Romans 5:1)
      4. Christ possesses and offers eternal life for all. (I John 5:11)

II. Behold . . . The Way Of Death
   A. Death is the result of sin.
      1. All have sinned and deserve death. (Romans 3:23)
      2. Sin is a growing thing in the heart and leads ever down to destruction. (James 1:15)
      3. The result of sin is sure death. (Romans 6:23)
   B. The death which results from sin is eternal.
      1. There are both judgment and existence beyond the grave. (Hebrews 9:27)
      2. Eternal death involves separation from God and has objective reality. (Revelation 20:11-15)

III. Behold . . . The Way Of Choice
   A. The very fact that two ways are set before mankind indicates that man has opportunity to make a choice.
   B. At the very time you hear these words, you face that choice.
      1. The road that leads to death has attributes which make it appear as the proper road. (Proverbs 14:12; 12:15; Matthew 7:13)
      2. Jesus Christ says, "I am the way, the truth and the life . . . " He has provided the way; all we need do is receive and follow Him.
   C. Right now you have opportunity to chose to leave the road of death and get on the road of life.
      1. All you need do is invite Jesus Christ into your

life for He has already provided everything you need for salvation.

2. Simply own up to your sins and believe on Him for salvation.

Conclusion:

Won't you accept Him as your Saviour and get off the road that leads to death and on the road which leads to everlasting life?

The hymnwriter said:

There's a Saviour who stands at the door of your heart,
He is longing to enter, why let Him depart?
He is patiently waiting your soul to receive,
But you must open the door.
You must open the door, You must open the door.
When Jesus comes in, He will save you from sin,
But you must open the door.

Three Men With A Problem

VARIOUS SCRIPTURES

Introduction:

The Bible abounds with living characters. Here we consider three of these living characters of the Bible who are united by a common fact — each had a problem.

As we look at these men, we will consider the problem, the way in which it was solved and the significance of the solution. In so doing we will also be drawing some applications.

I. **The Man Who Couldn't Do Anything Right (Mark 5:1-20)**
   A. His character:
      1. He was possessed of demons.
      2. He was in a deplorable condition.
      3. He was utterly beside himself.
   B. His case history:
      1. Came to Christ.
      2. Even in his awful state, he realized who Christ was.
   C. His cure:
      1. Christ cast out the demons.
      2. Man cleansed and restored to society.

II. **The Man Who Wanted To Do Right (John 3)**
   A. His character:
      1. He was a just and honest man.
      2. He was sufficiently good to be a "ruler" of the Jews.
   B. His case history:
      1. Came to Jesus under the cover of darkness.
      2. Asked the questions of an honest seeker after God.
   C. The cure:
      1. Christ showed him the way of eternal life.
      2. It appears that Nicodemus accepted and became a loyal follower of Jesus Christ (John 19:36).

III. **The Man Who Thought He Couldn't Do Anything Wrong (Galatians 1:13 & 14; Acts 9:1-16)**
   A. His character:
      1. Zealous for the things of God.
      2. A religionist of the religious.

B. His case history:
   1. Christ spoke to him in a special way.
   2. He showed a receptive heart.
C. His cure:
   1. Christ divinely filled his vision.
   2. He became one of God's mighty ones.

Conclusion:

The first man was down and out. He didn't realize his need until he got in contact with Christ, but once he did, he was helped in spite of his condition.

The second man had something lacking in his life and contact with Christ brought it out. He came to Christ, trying Him, to find the answer, and he found in Him reality of life.

The third man, a lifelong church member, thought he really had it. When he came to Christ, however, he discovered that he had never found true religion.

Each had a problem, each got to the right place and each had it solved in Jesus. Whatever your problem, Christ has the answer to the need of your soul.

Where To Look For Salvation
ISAIAH 45:22

Introduction:
The Bible says, "look unto me and be ye saved . . . " It is of tremendous importance that men know where to look if they are ever to be saved. This verse clearly shows just where it is that men are to look for salvation.

I. **God Is The Author Of Salvation**
   A. His wisdom drew the plan. It was a divine arrangement that the "seed of the woman should bruise the serpent's head."
   B. His love procured the sacrifice. "God so loved the world that He gave His only begotten Son . . . "
   C. His favor makes us heirs of salvation. "By grace are ye saved . . . "
   D. His Spirit seals the contract. "The Spirit itself beareth witness with our spirit that we are the children of God."

II. **God Desires The Salvation Of The Whole Human Race**
   A. The salvation which God offers is offered to the whole human race.
   B. The salvation which God offers is offered to every nation and country.
   C. The salvation which God offers is offered to every individual.
   D. This salvation is richly adapted to the wants of mankind everywhere and in every condition.

III. **God's Salvation Can Be Obtained From No Other Source**
   A. Man is totally unable to save himself.
   B. Man's friends are powerless to save him.
   C. Man's good works are not sufficient to save him.
   D. Man's church or church relationship can't save him.
   E. Even angels can't save man.

Conclusion:
God alone possesses the power to save. In what are you trusting for salvation? Jesus is our only Saviour, and He holds up His bleeding hands and says, "Look and live." Why not look to Him now? Why not look to Him now?

-Adapted from *Sketches of Revival Sermons*

Seeking The Lord

AMOS 5:6

Introduction:
Israel was, in the days of the Prophet Amos, wicked and rebellious. God saw that they were bringing wretchedness, ruin and death upon themselves as the result of their sinful conduct, hence He calls upon them to seek Him, assuring them that their condition, though lamentable, is not hopeless. These words are applicable to all who are living without hope and without God in this world.

I. **The Duty Urged - Seek The Lord**
   A. This implies that man has lost God.
   B. This implies that man must awaken to the consciousness of the fact that he has lost God. The Holy Spirit produces this consciousness.
   C. This implies earnest inquiry as to how the Lord may be found.
   D. This implies coming in God's own way.
      1. A confession of sin.
      2. A forsaking of sin.
      3. Faith in the Lord Jesus Christ.

II. **The Encouragement Given----And Ye Shall Live.**
   A. Sin has brought man under condemnation of sin - death. "Wherefore, as by one man sin entered into the world and death by sin; and so death passed upon all men for that all have sinned . . . "
   B. Divine grace delivers from this condemnation. "For if by one man's offence death reigned by one; much more they that receive abundance of grace, and of the gift of righteousness, shall reign in life by one, Jesus Christ."
   C. Divine grace delivers to a life that is full and free:
      1. In intimate communion with God.
      2. In the full exercise of God-given powers.
      3. For eternity.

Conclusion:
" . . . that whosoever believeth in Him should not perish, but have everlasting life."
"It is time to seek the Lord!!!"

- Adapted

The Sight At The Cross
MATTHEW 27:26, 33-51

Introduction:
Of the many that were present when Christ was crucified, we are told of some: "And sitting down, they watched Him there."

I. The Person At The Cross
    A. Crucifixion not a distinguishing death in itself.
    B. Note what distinguished this death:
        1. Refusal of sedation (33).
        2. Excessive physical punishment (26, 29).
        3. Prophetic superscription (37).
        4. Reaction in nature (45, 51b).
        5. Rending of the temple veil (51a).
    C. The man there is identified by the very mocking of the throng.
        1. A king.
        2. A saviour.
        3. The Son of God.

II. The Event At The Cross
    A. The culmination of history:
        1. Promises to Adam and Eve fulfilled (Genesis 3:15).
        2. The calling of Abraham consumated (Genesis 12:3).
        3. The purposes of Israel accomplished.
        4. Religious symbols and rites completed.
        5. Prophecy fulfilled.
    B. The cross becomes the focal point of subsequent history.
    C. The cross becomes the dividing line in spiritual experience.

III. The Victory At The Cross
    A. Satan's claims were paid.
    B. Christ's suffering was ended.
    C. Man's suffering was potentially ended in Christ.

IV. The People At The Cross
    A. A mocking, scorning throng (39 & 40).
    B. Blasphemous, scorning religious leaders (41-43).
    C. A doubting, scorning thief (44).

D. Fearfully adoring women (55).
E. The Roman soldiery:
    1. Before (27-31) worse than all others.
    2. After (54) convinced of just who He really was.

Conclusion:

We've seen the cross and the people who were there.

With which group of those there would you wish to be identified?

Why not accept the witness of the soldiers who were so impressed and receive Jesus into your heart?

When Faced With Jesus
MATTHEW 13:53-58

Introduction:

When faced with Jesus and His claims, everyone reacts in some way or another. The way in which His "hometown" folk reacted is very instructive.

I. The Background To The Story
   A. Return of the native to His own hometown after some months out in the larger world.
   B. People there must have heard of His exploits, etc.
   C. In returning, He followed the usual procedure of going into the synagogue on the Sabbath to read and comment upon the Scriptures.

II. The Claims Made In The Story: "This Day Is The Scripture Fulfilled In Your Ears."
   A. Claimed a divine commissioning:
      1. Said He was sent of God.
      2. Said He was possessed of the Spirit in full measure.
      3. Said He was annointed of God.
   B. Claimed divine purposes:
      1. To preach the Gospel to the poor (the spiritually impoverished).
      2. To heal the brokenhearted (those broken by sin's calamities).
      3. To preach deliverance to the captives (those in bondage to Satan).
      4. To preach the recovering of sight to the blind (those in spiritual darkness).
      5. To set at liberty the bruised (those fettered and deeply hurt by Satan).
      6. To preach the acceptable year of the Lord.

III. The Reactions Recorded In The Story
   A. Astonishment
      1. Struck with wonder at the grace of His person and words.
      2. Began to center their amazement on His person.
   B. Questioning
      1. Where did He get all this power?
      2. Where did He get this wisdom?
      3. Isn't this just the carpenter's son?

4. Isn't He just one of us here?
5. Where does He get the airs He is putting on?
C. Offense
1. They were offended at His words.
2. They grew angry at Him.
3. They sought to destroy Him (people often seek to destroy what they can't handle otherwise).

IV. Implications
A. He still makes the same claims:
1. He claims to be sent from God.
2. He claims the same purposes:
a. Preach the Gospel.
b. Heal broken hearts.
c. Bring deliverance.
d. Give sight to spiritually blind.
e. Free the bound.
f. Commend the moment as the time.
B. Men still react:
1. Many are astonished.
2. Many question.
3. Many are offended.

Conclusion:

Faced with Jesus, men long ago were forced to take some action or define some stands. Men are still faced by Christ today, and they are still forced to face issues by that facing.

The way in which you react to Jesus Christ will determine your eternal destiny.

Seeking Christ

MARK 1:37

Introduction:

Man is a seeker of many things by nature. There is a mysterious personal quality about some men that leads other men to seek them. So it was with the Lord Jesus Christ when He was here on earth.

Even today there are men who seek after Christ when they are spiritually awakened and attracted by the Gospel and influenced by the Holy Spirit.

I. **What In Men Leads Them To Seek Christ?**
    A. Curiosity leads some men to seek Him.
        1. Many followed Him when He was here because they were curious about His ministry and work.
        2. Many today follow Him because they are curious about things they have seen and heard concerning Him.
    B. Admiration leads some men to seek Him.
        1. Some were attracted to Him while He was on earth by His matchless character of purity and holiness.
        2. Some men today are attracted by the high moral standard of Christianity.
    C. Need for release for suffering leads some men to seek Him.
        1. Many of those who came to Him while He was on earth came because they had specific needs which they felt He could supply.
        2. Many men come to Him today because of the fact that they need help in facing some serious problem.
    D. Sin and a sense of needed pardon leads some men to seek Him.
        1. Many of those who came to Him while He was on earth were under a burdensome load of sin and despair.
        2. Many men come to Him today because they sense a need for release from guilt and the weight of sin.

II. **What In Christ Leads Men To Seek Him?**
    A. The fact that He seeks them.

45

1. He came to "Seek and to save the lost."
2. If we love Him, it is because He first loved us.
B. His invitations and promises:
1. He has bidden men to seek His help and assured them that they will not seek in vain.
2. He says, "Come unto me . . . and ye shall find rest to your souls."
C. His power to respond to their appeals:
1. Those who keep seeking and failing to find anything are discouraged from further seeking.
2. He is always found of those who diligently seek Him.

III. How Should Men Seek Christ?
A. Sincerely and seriously.
B. In faith
C. At the accepted time which is right now.

Conclusion:

Man is a seeker by nature. There are certain qualities in man and certain qualities in Christ which would cause a man to seek Him. "Seek ye the Lord while He may be found."

-Adapted from *Sketches of Revival Sermons*

To The Uttermost

HEBREWS 7:25

Introduction:

There are many remedies for the maladies of man which are nothing more than "half-way" measures which alleviate without curing. The work done by Jesus Christ is no "half-way" measure, but it something which cares for man's problem of sin to the uttermost.

I. **Christ Is Able To Save Sinners**
   A. He was authorized by God to do so.
   B. He was qualified both by His divine nature and His experiences of life to deal with sin for He knew sinners and He knew sin by divine observation.
   C. He removed the great obstacle to salvation - sin. He is a saviour because He became a sin-bearer.
   D. He had a loving heart which was willing to do what was needed.
   E. He was long accustomed to the work. The decision had been made in eternity past and comprehended by Him as if already accomplished.

II. **This Salvation Is "To The Uttermost"**
   A. It is a salvation for extreme sinners. No matter how low one has fallen, he has not fallen below His ability to rescue.
   B. It is a salvation for extreme sins.
      1. It is a salvation from *any* sin at all.
      2. It is a salvation from *every* sin.
   C. It is a salvation in uttermost circumstances. Even peculiarly grievous cases which have been given up by man are comprehended in His divine ability.
   D. It is a salvation to the uttermost extent of salvation.
      1. Perfect reconciliation - all past forgotten.
      2. Perfect purity - all charges and spots removed.
   E. It is a salvation to eternity.

III. **This Salvation Is Open To Any Sinner Who Comes To God By Christ**
   A. The explanation:
      1. "Coming to God" means true repentance.
      2. "By Him" means real faith in Him and His work.
   B. The exhortation:
      1. You need a saviour sorely.

2. There is no other Saviour beside Jesus.
3. You are ruined if you don't accept Him.
C. The encouragement:
1. The text implies a wonderful fact, that you may come to God.
2. This salvation will prove an enormous blessing to the one coming.

Conclusion:

The work of salvation is a perfect work. All it lacks for absolute perfection as far as you are concerned is your reception of Christ as Saviour.

-Adapted from *Sketches of Revival Sermons*

The Gospel In A Verse
I TIMOTHY 1:15

Introduction:

We usually use too many words to say too few things. There is a place in the Bible, however, where the Spirit of God directed the Apostle Paul to say about as much in about as few words as possibly could be said. Notice the Gospel in a verse.

I. **A Broad Word Of Description - Sinners**
   A. Includes sinners of all sorts.
   B. Includes sinners in all their polution.
   C. Includes sinners without strength who are under the curse.
   D. This is just a plain reference to sinners without other qualification.

II. **A Wide Word Of Salvation - To Save**
   A. There are several things Christ did not come to do:
      1. He did not come to condemn us.
      2. He did not come to help us save ourselves.
      3. He did not come to save us in part.
      4. He did not come to make us remain content unsaved.
      5. He did not come just to save sinners from the punishment of their sins.
   B. There are things He did come to do:
      1. He came to save sinners from the polution of their sins.
      2. He came to free sinners from the tendency and necessity of sins.

III. **A Glorious Word Of Honor - Christ Jesus**
   A. The name Jesus means "Saviour".
   B. The name Christ means "annointed one."

IV. **A Sure Word Of Fact - Came Into The World**
   A. It is an historic fact that He came into the world.
   B. He had existed long before He came. His coming was just a change of form rather than a beginning of existence.
   C. His coming was willing and voluntary.
   D. He came and stayed long enough to complete His entire work.

V. A Personal Word Of Decision - Worthy Of All Acceptation

A. We need to confess our sinful state.
B. We need to be humbled before Him by all He has done.
C. We need to appropriate Him by faith.
D. We need to openly confess Him as our Saviour and Lord.

Conclusion:

Have you ever taken this step and made this decision? Here is the Gospel in a verse. Now the need is to write the Gospel in your heart.

- Adapted from C.H. Spurgeon

The Twofold Possession
I JOHN 5:12

Introduction:

The life of which the Apostle John so often speaks is spiritual and eternal. It pertains to the soul and denotes the blessedness of the soul of one who truly believes in the Son of God.

The true believer has a twofold possession — he has Christ and in Him he has life spiritual and eternal.

All depends on our relation to Christ. Without Him we are dead in sin; with Him, we are united to God in life.

I. What Does It Mean To Have The Son?
   A. Having the Son of God means that we know Him.
      1. This is more than a vague intellectual acquaintance with Him.
      2. It means a close, intimate knowledge of His person and character.
   B. Having Christ means a spiritual reception of Him by faith.
      1. True faith accepts Jesus Christ and has Him in the truest sense.
      2. Christ dwells in the believing heart.
   C. Having Christ means that we draw upon Him.
      1. He is the bread of life on which we feed.
      2. He is the foundation of life on which we build.
   D. Having Christ means that we voluntarily give ourselves up to Him.

II. What Is The Life Which We Have Through The Son Of God?
   A. Freedom from condemnation.
      1. We are justified fully and freely when we have Christ.
      2. There is no one who can tamper with what Christ has purchased for Himself.
   B. Peace with God.
   C. Communion with God and the sense of His favor.
      1. Man's fellowship with God was destroyed by sin. Now it is restored for those who have Christ.
      2. Now our fellowship is with the Father and the Son.
   D. The love of God in the heart.

1. This will produce in us love for God.
2. This will also produce in us love for our fellow man.
E. Holy joy. This is a deep, satisfying sense of spiritual rejoicing.
F. The hope of eternal blessedness in His presence.

Conclusion:

Are you alive now? Are you really living now? Only the person who has the Son can know the real meaning of living.

-Adapted from Charlesworth

Blinded By Satan

II CORINTHIANS 4:4

Introduction:

Just as a man may be physically blind, he may also be spiritually blind in spite of knowledge of the Bible, an acquaintance with the things of God and a head knowledge of spiritual things. The problem is lack of heart knowledge because he knows none of these things by experience.

I. **This Blindness Is Very Common**
   A. It shows itself in many ways:
      1. Occupation with this world and all that is in it.
      2. The easy conscience of many.
      3. The fact that many are almost looking for opportunities to sin.
      4. The way in which so many triffle with sin.
   B. Many people today have presumptuous hopes about the future without ever troubling themselves to make ready for it.

II. **This Blindness Is Satan-Induced In Various Ways**
   A. Some he blinds by worldliness and the quest for living.
   B. Others are blinded by love of some favorite secret sin.
   C. Still others are blinded by following the group, by failure to break with the direction of the crowd.
   D. Some are blinded by repeatedly raising objections to spiritual truth.
   E. Some are blinded by false inferences drawn from actual truth.
   F. Some are blinded by the god of intellectual attainment.
   G. Still others are blinded by false concepts of grace.

III. **The Kind Of Treatment This Blindness Requires**
   A. Blindness of heart is not only a sin but also a punishment for sin. It so often results in a hardened conscience.
   B. If you have even a little spiritual sight, value and cultivate it seriously.
   C. To be rid of spiritual blindness, we must admit that we suffer from it and confess it to God.
   D. Trust the Lord to open your blinded eyes so you may see again.

Conclusion:

There are many blind people who do not use a cane or a seeing-eye dog. Their spiritual vision is unobscured, but their spiritual eyes are stone blind. May God grant you to see things spiritually.

- Adapted from C.H. Spurgeon

The Free Gift Of God

ROMANS 5:15, 16, 18

Introduction:

The greatest philanthropist the world has ever known is our Heavenly Father. He has given more and given greater than any man who has ever lived. Let's look at His great gift.

I. **The Giver Of The Gift - God**
   - A. He is the God of peace (verse 1).
   - B. He is the God of glory (verse 2).
   - C. He is the God of love (verses 5-8).
   - D. He is the God of reconciliation (verse 10).
   - E. He is the God of joy (verse 11).
   - F. He is the God of grace (verse 15).

II. **The Grace Of The Gift - Jesus Christ**
   - A. He was the gift that had been promised (Genesis 12:3-7 and Galatians 3:16).
   - B. He was the most precious gift. (I Peter 2:7).
   - C. He was the providing gift, for He has provided:
     1. Peace with God (verse 1).
     2. Access to God (verse 2).
     3. Joy of hope (verse 2).
     4. The Holy Spirit (verse 5).
     5. Salvation (verses 6, 8-10).
     6. Eternal life (verse 21).
     7. Justification (verses 1-9).

III. **The Ground Of The Gift - The Grace Of God**
   - A. The source of this grace is in God.
   - B. The subjects of grace are:
     1. The strengthless (verse 6).
     2. The sinner (verse 8).
     3. The enemy of God (verse 10).
     4. The person dead in sin (verse 12).
     5. The condemned (verse 18).
     6. The disobedient (verse 19).
     7. The separated (verse 11).
   - C. The standing of grace is on a sure standing place (verse 2).
   - D. The supply of grace is abundant (verse 17).
   - E. The surmounting of this grace is that it is "much more" (verse 20).
   - F. The submission of this grace is so that grace might

reign (verse 21).

IV. The Glory Of The Gift - Hath Abounded Unto Many

   A. The gift of God is something which has had enormous outreach. It has not been limited to just a few over the span of history.

   B. The gift of God is available today to the man who is willing to seek it and receive it.

V. The Gratuitousness Of The Gift - The Free Gift Of God

   A. There is no price tag on the gift of God except what Christ has already paid for the sins of mankind.

   B. This is a gift freely given which must be freely received.

Conclusion:

Paul says: "He that spared not His own Son, but delivered Him up for us all, how shall He not with Him also freely give us all things."

- Adapted

Conditions Of Being Saved
ACTS 16:30

Introduction:
The question asked so long ago, "What must I do to be saved?" still echoes today. There are so many answers being given that it might be well to examine just exactly what answer the Bible gives to the question.

I. **What Sinners Must Not Do To Be Saved**
   A. They must not misunderstand just what is required for salvation.
   B. They must not say or imagine they cannot do what God requires.
   C. They must not procrastinate.
   D. They must not sit by and wait for God to do what He has commanded them to do.
   E. They must not flee to any refuge of lies.
   F. They must not seek for any self-indulgent or self-help method of salvation.
   G. They must not imagine they will have a more favorable time.
   H. They must not wait to see what others will do or say in regard to salvation.

II. **What Sinners Must Do To Be Saved**
   A. They must understand that they need to be saved.
   B. They must return and confess their sins to God.
   C. They must renounce themselves. This involves:
      1. Renunciation of one's own righteousness.
      2. Relinquishing of the idea that one has done enough good to commend himself to God on that basis.
      3. Renunciation of one's own will.
      4. Renunciation of one's own way.
   D. They must come to Christ and accept Him as personal Saviour.
   E. They must seek supremely to please Christ and not self.
   F. They must have full confidence in Christ's ability to save.
   G. They must forsake all to follow Christ.

Conclusion:
Take care that you do not sin willfully after having

understood the truth concerning the plan of salvation.

Do not wait even to go home before you obey God. Make up your mind right now and at once accept the offer of salvation.

You have now been told what you must not do and what you must do to be saved. Are you prepared to act?

- Adapted from C.G. Finney

What Must I Do To Be Saved?

ACTS 16:30, 31

Introduction:

Here is an age-old question asked by nearly everyone who has ever had opportunity to really hear the Gospel. What must I do to be saved?

I. A Question - What Must I Do To Be Saved?
  A. First asked by an anxious inquirer.
     1. He was one who wanted to know the truth.
     2. He was one who had realized that he was lost.
     3. He was one who knew that he needed some kind of salvation.
     4. He was one who had already discovered that he couldn't save himself by any available means.
  B. It was a question which demanded an honest answer.
     1. The answer needed most was a Scriptural answer.
     2. The answer needed to be one that would get to the heart of the problem.
  C. It was a question asked to one who knew the answer and in whom the questioner had confidence.

II. An Answer - Believe On The Lord Jesus Christ!!
   This involves at least six things:
  A. One must have heard the Gospel (Romans 10:17).
  B. One must seek the Lord (Matthew 11:28).
  C. One must repent of sins (Acts 17:30).
  D. One must be converted (Matthew 18:3).
  E. One must believe in Christ (Mark 1:15).
  F. One must be born again (John 3:3, 5, 7).

III. A Promise - Thou Shalt Be Saved
  A. Salvation is defined as the act of saving, preserving from destruction, danger or calamity.
  B. Biblically, it is the redemption of man from the bondage of sin and liability to eternal death, and the conferring on him of eternal happiness.

Conclusion:

It is an age-old question with a simple answer. Another question is in order, however, and that is, "Have you done what you must to be saved?"

- Adapted

The Gift Of God

ROMANS 6:23

Introduction:

From this text we may learn the freeness and the preciousness of the salvation revealed in the Gospel. It is called a gift to denote its freeness; it is called life on account of its inestimable value. Because it is a blessing of the most enduring kind, it is called eternal life.

I. **Notice The Gift**
   A. God's gifts to man are many and great. All that tends to enrichment and comfort is from the bounty of his Maker.
   B. There is one gift of God which transcends all others and which is received through faith in Jesus Christ - the gift of eternal life.
      1. This brings with it all the blessings and privileges which believers in Christ now enjoy by virtue of their union with Him.
      2. This will bring with it all the blessings of heaven.

II. **This Gift Is Freely Bestowed**
   A. Notice that it is a *gift*.
   B. It is not obtained by merit or earning but received as a gift.
   C. Faith is the condition rather than works because sinners are saved by grace alone.
   D. Even though salvation must be sought, it is still a gift.

III. **This Gift Comes Through Christ**
   A. We are saved for His sake.
   B. God gave His Son to redeem us, and now He gives us by His Spirit a personal, conscious interest in the blessings of redemption.
   C. To receive God's gift, we must receive His Son in faith.

Conclusion:

"To as many as received Him, to them gave He the power to become the Sons of God, even to them that believe in His name."

Faith receives Christ, God's gift to man, and obtains eternal life in Him.

-Adapted from Charlesworth

The Prodigal's Resolve
LUKE 15:18

Introduction:
This young man, the son of a rich Jew, was thoroughly destitute. He was hungry and in rags. Seated amid the swine troughs, perfectly wretched, an idea flashes across him, "I will go home. These are no clothes for a rich man's son to wear. What business is this for a Jew, feeding swine? I can stand it no longer. I will arise and go to my Father."

I. **This Resolution Was Made In Disgust At His Present Condition**
   A. It was because he had come to his lowest point that he made the decision to return home.
   B. Few men ever start for God without conviction of their famine-struck condition.

II. **This Resolution Was Formed In Sorrow For His Past Behaviour**
   A. Behind the physical privation which motivated him lay concern for what he had done in the past (this was revealed in his confession upon returning home).
   B. There needs to be an element of sorrow in our coming to the Lord. We must view our situation as sinfully affecting Him.

III. **This Resolution Was Formed In A Time Of Homesickness**
   A. This young man had been gone long enough to be very homesick for his father and home.
   B. There are many men today who are homesick for God and heaven.

IV. **This Resolution Was Immediately Put Into Operation**
   A. Many resolutions are not carried out, but we read that this young man made his decision and then immediately arose and carried it out.
   B. The man who senses his need ought to make his move right at the moment when he senses his need.

Conclusion:
Why will you starve in the desert when you might feast in your Father's house? God wants you to come back. Angels want you to come back. The church wants you to come back.

- Adapted from *Sketches of Revival Sermons*

Despising God

I SAMUEL 2:30

Introduction:

In the general disregard for God we find about us, there is strong evidence that there are some who genuinely despise God. This may be for various reasons or for no reason whatever. The Bible has something to day about this matter of despising God.

I. **The Being Whom Sinners Despise**
   A. He is the Almighty King of the universe.
   B. He is the One who is:
      1. Their creator.
      2. Their benefactor.
      3. Their redeemer.

II. **The Ways In Which Sinners Despise God**
   A. By refusing to acknowledge His authority.
      1. Some deny that God even exists.
      2. Others admit the reality of His existence but deny it in practice by the way in which they refuse to consider or respect the principles of His government.
   B. By not heeding His gracious call to repentance and faith in the Lord Jesus Christ.
   C. By making light of the means of grace.
      1. Ignore the Lord's Day.
      2. Reject the Bible.
      3. Absent themselves from the service of His house.
      4. Scoff at the idea of prayer.
      5. Rebel against the ordinances of His church.
   D. By despising His people.

III. **The Reward Of Despising God**
   A. He shall be despised of God:
      1. In not being recognized as a child of God. Although he may know great esteem and honor in the world, the greatest honor is withheld from him.
      2. In his own eyes when conscience is aroused. In days of prosperity, the wicked are unconcerned as to what God thinks of them, but when adversity befalls them, the sleeping conscience is aroused

and they begin to see themselves as God sees them.

B. He shall be despised in the day of judgment. "Depart from me, ye cursed." Disowned by God, they will go their way with shame into the eternal punishment of hell.

Conclusion:

Men can and do despise God. The price of such despite, however, is that of being despised in return by God Himself.

- Adapted

Not Rich Toward God

LUKE 12:21

Introduction:

Riches and poverty are relative values. Some of the richest men in the world are actually poverty stricken while some of the poorest by material standards are among the richest. No man is rich, however, until he is rich toward God.

I. **Who Is He That Is Rich Before God?**
   - A. He that is rich in the estimation of God.
   - B. He that is rich in favor with God.
   - C. He that is rich in the grace which God imparts.
   - D. He that is rich in a title to the promised inheritance.

II. **Who Is He That Is Rich Toward Himself?**
   - A. He whose ruling passion is the accumulation of worldly wealth.
   - B. He who expends his wealth only for his own gratification.

III. **Where Lies The Folly Of The Man Not Rich Toward God?**
   - A. His wealth does not make him happy.
   - B. His wealth may be snatched away from him.
   - C. His wealth must be resigned at death.
   - D. His wealth must be exchanged hereafter for treasures of vengeance.

IV. **What Should Be Our Personal Application Of These Things?**
   - A. To the man not rich toward God - how unhappy is the reality of the state in which he finds himself.
   - B. To the unconverted man - how urgent the need for better blessings than this world can bring.
   - C. To the Christian - how thankful he should be for the better and more enduring substance.
   - D. To all men - how desirable it is that we should desire above all else to be rich toward God.

Conclusion:

It is not always easy to determine whether or not an individual is truly rich. Each one, however, knows whether or not he is rich toward God.

- Adapted